D0540216

WHO GOES THERE?

Penny Boxall was born in 1987. Her debut collection of poetry, *Ship of the Line*, was first published in 2014 and relaunched in a new edition by Valley Press in 2018. She won the 2016 Edwin Morgan Poetry Award and the Elmet Trust Competition, and holds an MA with distinction in Creative Writing (Poetry) from UEA. In 2017, she became writer-in-residence at Gladstone's Library in Flintshire and a Hawthornden Fellow.

Who Goes There?

PENNY BOXALL

Valley Press

First published in 2018 by Valley Press
Woodend, The Crescent, Scarborough, YO11 2PW
www.valleypressuk.com

First edition, first printing (August 2018)

ISBN 978-1-912436-06-4
Cat. no. VP0126

Cover photograph by Rich Vintage Photography.
Cover design by Jamie McGarry. Text design by Jo Haywood.
Edited by Martha Sprackland.

Printed and bound in the EU by Pulsio, Paris.

Contents

Acknowledgements

These poems, or versions of them, have appeared in: *Gutter, The North, Mslexia, Magma, The Literateur, The Welsh Poetry Competition Anthology 2015, The Fenland Reed.*

Thanks:

For wisdom in Oxford, particularly to Brian, Alan and Charlotte.

To everyone who balanced friendship with editing, especially Rebecca Watts, James Midgley and Jane Boxall.

To encouragers: Rebecca Stott; Andrew Murray (again); Phil, Rob, Jean and Anthony; Steph; Evie and family; the Boxalls and Langfords; and James.

I am deeply grateful to the judges and trustees of the 2016 Edwin Morgan Poetry Award for giving me the time and space to write; to Gladstone's Library for a residency in August 2017; and to Hawthornden Castle for a Fellowship in November 2017.

for my relatives

Caretaking

Unbereaved, there's time to take things in:
the lumbering organ like a gentle beast

and the undertakers' private nods, small
movements each for something separate.

My friend the priest is doing his best
to make them a whole. I watch the wall

of his back, the barrier of the gathered,
the arrangement of lilies on the coffin.

They sum her up: her laugh,
her wicked sense of fun.

One girl reads a comic rhyme and doesn't cry.
The mourners laugh at the relief.

The Mourners, as though
characters drawn from a pool.

This set will never congregate
again, not in this arrangement,

with the sun sifting through high glass
this bright November day; and me

in my discreet position should anything go wrong –
should anything additional and curable go wrong.

The Knocker-Upper

Deep breath, then spit
the pellet
through the straw
to the window.
To raise the dead
at fifty paces: god!

The backstreets
spread, a blackened map.
Ping! That's the baker up
and rising, a reluctant loaf.
The tailor greets me sharp
as needles

but I'm gone
to the fishmonger and his thin
wife, pouring stink
from their scaled garret.
I strike iron into the heart
of the smith.

The day shows itself
like a stain on linen. Each pea
blazes on a quick
tangent, comets
in the growing sky.

One pea I'll never shoot:
deep in my apron pocket,
my desert island bullet.
It's what gets me up –
its tiny potential
fit to burst.

Appetite

The peel tumbles from the bowl,
an invitation. There is already
a brown stain on the head
of a middle-aged apple.

Tulips droop at the thought.
Striped mistresses, they shred
themselves like letters
slipped in the night.

The wine in its glass holds
ground beside the knife,
the opened skull and butterfly.
Snipe are limp on the sill.

The too-ripe lobster on its salver
gathers flies like compliments.
Give me three glossy cobnuts
and that fat peach, blowing over.

Dr Johnson's Wasp

'A brisk stinging insect, in form resembling a bee.'
Samuel Johnson, A Dictionary of the English Language (1775)

They are at the long table, each busy in his mind.
    A wasp taps again and again against the window.
Of all parts of the world it could have filled with its half-inch
    the wasp has chosen this lofty room, full of work.
They are perfecting meaning on a line – trying
    to catch their words and pin them down.
They are working on *W*, which stands for many things
    (*wanderer, wastrel, workshy, when* and *why*).
The wasp wears its nipped livery like a footman.
    If a man could hear anything outside his mind
the wasp's clockwork *tink* against the glass could let itself in,
    reveal as its cause this brisk insect, so unlike a bee.

Workbox

John Craske (1881-1943) came from a long line of fishermen,
but ill health prevented him from going to sea. Instead, he embroidered it.

No work for a man, this endless redoing,
this close-work, this stump-work, this crewel.
Pins are for pinning, for sticking and fixing
the thorax, the eye-brightened wing –
for forcing through maps, for defining a front.
Pins are for bearing up bones when you've smashed
through a fence on a – yes – on a hair-pin.
Pins means her legs and that's all there is to it.

Needles are bloodletters, drugpushers, Christmas,
the spark between silence and song. Hide needles
in hayricks and think yourself lucky
you're not the one looking, you're too busy coaxing
this shapeshifting camel to go where it's told –
but boy, above all, you're not bloody sewing.

Nails are for nailing and shoeing and roofing.
Nails are for boots and the Cross.

Silks are for weddings, for smallclothes, for secrets,
for never-you-minds and not-for-your-eyes.
No business with silks, with unravelling
skeins, with spooling, with winding,
with twist versus floss.

And man, you're a piece of work anyway.
Consider your beard, your pièce de résistance,
your tangling mass, your miraculous haul.
It's thick with the threads that you spun for yourself,
that you wove though you didn't know how.

Godwit's Silhouette

Jeremy Godwit, b. 1770; lost 1826

He was the only Godwit in the parish:
the registrar, distracted by some clamour
outside the church, mislabelled him,
morphed the *n* into a *t* and forced
a new horizon to the name.

*

Sturdy as a stork, he had a shade
for everything. He knew his mind;
would steer you to the blues and greens to flatter,
dissuade you from the reds you thought became you.
Clothes make the man, he'd chime, not adding
if Godwit wills. That much was understood.
Glasses perched, he waited,
patient, for your change of heart.
He'd fling out yards of fabric
and, seen through them, briefly change –
a soft impression of a shape
behind the muslin sprigs, the flocking –
until you called him back,
dispelled the notion cloth had entertained.

*

We found his suit laid out and ready,
the day we lost him.
He wasn't to be found inside its folds,
nor tidied neatly on the dark wood shelves.
No shroud was needed, since there was no gent.
We took to the shore, raked shells
like code, and did not find an answer
underneath the flapping cloud
till someone chanced it: 'If there's blue
enough to make a sailor's trousers...'
Then we knew.

King of the Folly

I scoured the *Globe*, the *List* and the *Gazette*
for situations vacant these last months.
The search near fruitless, I had almost quit
before unwontedly I scored this plum,
this golden possibility, this peach.
The masters like the hours I keep (quite none)
and stipulate the levels of decay
to propagate. They like the look – the thought –
of me, the wildman in the foliage,
a visitor unvisiting, unkempt.

They built this wilderness: forced gunpowder
to blast from wordless ground a fitting art,
and summoned springs where nothing welled before.
My home will be decrepit, dank, just so.
They scooped a rock out for me, sunk the grass,
erected statues to the living dead;
then brought in chicken bones to rake the mud,
commissioned shells from coasts I've never seen
to foster sounds, like small abandoned caves.
I barely look at them, my mind's eye full
with truths which I'd do better to forget.
Thus set, I'll live in visions; I'll invent
more proper observations to report.

I know my place and peer out from the tomb
as Jesus must have done, though I've the gift
of time. They come here full of faith and I
can't disappoint. They're certain, for their coin,
to spot sublime reflections in the dark.
Memento mori realised in flesh:
they carve initialled hearts and then vacate.

I'm served my daily porridge from a skull.
How do I live for loneliness? Just think.
I'm less a fellow than belief; a piece
of theatre scenery, a prop.

Am I the gardener? No, madame – he's waged:
a young man from the village I once knew
but now ignore. For sure, I sneak at dusk
sometimes, kill time among the hops, scoff pork
(the which my contract certainly forbids);
but I'm a careful occupant of night,
make sure I'm back by dawn, my garments creased
in places my superiors approve,
my whiskers freshly dirtied, eyes set wild.

The mornings are my best times. I awake
to birdsong and the sound of air.
The rain I relish, too; a physical
exertion of God's immanence, a hint.
It alters all, releases that strange smell
– though 'smell' is not the word – and pricks the earth
with loveliness: an inward pulse like nothing
in the world. It makes my hair stand up. I live
in these huge moments of capacity –
my plot, my furtherment, my little will.

Henry Acland's Box

'…the fish had been packed in salt and placed in an eight-foot-long box addressed to 'Dr Acland, Oxford'. During the voyage, the crew and passengers had become convinced that the box contained a corpse, which in their superstitious minds was sufficient to account for the storm in the Bay of Biscay.'
Natural History Museum, Oxford

Dr Acland has expired.
We know this by

the brass plate
screwed on the man-sized box.

Dr Acland swears blue
this is not the case.

Bad luck reeks
from the four corners.

We hoist the shifting
weight toward a wet burial.

Dr Acland nips between us
and the sea – That is my box.

We agree, tipping it at the horizon.
No, no no no, he insists.

We tilt it back to deck.
Dr Acland jimmies a crowbar

between us and the answer:
a stink of wet salt; a gill like

a letterbox; a vagrant eye
and flabbergasted, wordless lips.

That is your box, we shout,
scattering to the wind.

This Way Up

My aim is Australia.
Disregard the obstacles, the fact
that my antipodes is actually
an unlanded Pacific plot.
Between me
and Uluru the Earth's core
pounds like a jealous heart.

I am pulled by my opposite,
determined to fling
the matter over my shoulders,
building a slow hill.

I cut into the stacked
cake of soils, rocks, roots
all the way to dinnertime; then abandon
my three-foot depth of ambition.

Unfulfilled, the rain tricks
its way in, far-reaching;
infiltrates bedrock and the star
at the heart of the planet;
down until there is no more

down and rain becomes a willing
upsurge, a welling into
heat. It sparks into the Bush,
conjures a flourishing of leaves
exotic to an unthinkable place:

crocuses, narcissi, violets extruding,
alien, into Down Under. Morning glory
translates to a pernicious weed,
bright as a seam to mine; so that the farmer,

led by his flock and no map
to that place, might be forgiven
for thinking he has discovered the source
of some huge, unimaginable richness.

Relocation

I. MOTHERING SUNDAY

In trains
        everywhere girls
                transport armfuls
                        of blooms
                                towards their
                                        future selves

II. BIG YELLOW SELF STORAGE

I think to myself (as I box up another untenable memory)
it's not *youth* that's wasted on the young, but experience –

III. THE TREASURE ACT

When we acquired
the glass ladybird
(twisted in tissue
carried home overseas
prized in its tiny cabinet)

I didn't expect
years later to find it
stuck in the fat of my foot
as I gave the room
a final once-over
with the hoover

IV. DATA PROTECTION

Thrusting scrunched
fists of
contextless scraps
into damp
paper banks
the soft
brushes at
the bin-mouths
catch my
evacuating hands

The Prophet Hen of Leeds

As fast as eggs are made they are
unlaid, pushed back up embellished
by Mary Bateman's acid pen. She sears
this legend into shell:

       Christ is coming, Christ is coming, Christ is –

The startled hen announces Armageddon
with its arse. It doesn't know which way
is up: no sooner has it birthed
the world than genesis reverses, sucked back
through the chute and home to dark. It does not know

why labour's never done and why

no effort it can muster comes to owt.

Soon every lay grows its own audience.

Mary dips her quill.
Each pen will only eke
so many omens out before it eats itself,
acid making light work of the tools.
But her message will outlast the means to make it.

Magnet

Rhythm brings worms blind and writhing
from the ground. They'll go to desperate lengths
for rain. Really, it's a dirty trick,

so I was pleased to see you this morning,
magnet dangling from your hand
and swinging little circles on its string.
This was dowsing of a sort. White buds
erupted where you'd been, hoodwinking
the first birds, happily, into spring.

The Valentine

A bolt that couldn't stand the test;
ball bearings, easing nothing now;
a pearly heart emblazoned *Best*:
its partner, *Friends*, is underground.
A bottleneck drained of its drink;
an ex-balloon with no breath left;
a hinge without a door; a sock;
a gap-toothed zip; a polished rock;
a battered tin; a rusted pin;
a key that never knew a lock.

An earthworm worried from the loam
and stretched long as my arm.
A baby tooth worked from the gum
and ceded to my palm.
A line torn from a Get Well card;
a hairball wrested from a hedge;
a gold toothpick; a mangled chick:
he's rooting for my heart.

Visitation

May, and the vestry's plagued
with them – little detachments
raising and reinterring
like defective Lazaruses.
I clock the underbelly of a chair
diffused by busy mouthparts,
wool erased with two years' blind
hunger that halts at manmade fibre.
The priest calls for intervening forces:
men in overalls who will raise
the stakes and blast the suckers dead.
Fifty centigrade: as hot or more so,
we agree, than hell.
(I watch one inch under
the cope chest and resolve.)

*

The van arrives quiet,
orderly. They disable smoke alarms,
fill the offices with fumes. Once-white
vestments relinquish their secrets. The whole
affair's in disarray, wedding records toppling
ecclesiastic silver, lost property bunched
round vials of chrism. The act itself only
takes a minute. Regardless, come Monday
the critters are still crawling from the
cracks, and not only our intended:
the method's universal. Behind the door
a cohort of silverfish lies gasping
on the lino, antennae pivoting as if still
expecting rescue, still hoping for a miracle.

The Animal Trials

The accused is a plague   of gnats
       hatched
              like a plot
       in the air
              of the abbey
It has swarmed with dark
       purpose
choked the prayers
              of the revolted
       devotees   It has moved on mysterious
updrafts   and gathered
       to the bent   heads stagnating
              thoughts
       It has entered
into mouths   reformed itself
       as hateful words
              Each gnat   small as a mote
                     contains
a portion of the devil   John the Mild
       has excommunicated
       the swarm –
              and it   will be
extinguished
              Tomorrow   the abbey
       floor   will lie thick
                     with tiny deaths
       final as full-stops
              We have engaged
       a char
to sweep the place   clean
       when she knocks   at the gate
we must
              let her in

28

The Warning Man

appears in perilous moments –
the flooded towpath, the greased road,
the recently mopped floor.
Nothing works out for him.
If he runs he skids, if he jumps he
splats. The black blot of his face
can read surprise or resignation
depending on how you look at it.
Why me? you can almost hear him wail
as he writhes on wet lino, legs out of order –
our slapstick scapegoat.
He shouldn't even think about
getting into that clifftop car.
On the platform he's stumped again
by steps, life too fast, arms straining
away from the thing that hounds him
straight into the next disaster.

Burnt Milk

A thickened skin
The cup reshelved

Go empty all the way to bed

A Flap-Dragon

Don't 'ee fear him but be bold –
Out he goes his flames are cold,
Snip! Snap! Dragon!
– trad.

The girls gather round the match
as it tips. The brandy buds into fire.
The bowl brims with blue light.
The boldest girl snatches quick as a flash – plucks
the little searing prize – and with her mouth
snuffs it out. She'll marry first.

The others eddy and shoal, nipping in,
claiming, singeing the skin of their lips.
The circle spreads outwards,
dimming until it seems
as if those lost to the gloom –
missing their chance –
aren't even trying.

Local News

A Ravensburger
jigsaw of the world
has exploded
on the Cowley Road.

No one will admit
they dropped it.
We do not invite
conflict.

Three days later
(the smash of motors
approximating tremors/
reassessing borders/
the territory reordered)
we are no closer
to an answer.

Operation Mincemeat

In April 1943, a disinformation strategy ('Operation Mincemeat') was implemented by the British Government: invent a Royal Marines Captain, and deposit his body, carrying false invasion plans, in the sea, to be washed up in a pro-Nazi Spanish village. Everything he carried – including a photograph of his invented fiancée, 'Pam' – was designed to mislead. It worked.

Even the bathing-suit was counterfeit. I slipped behind a dune and squeezed into the borrowed wool, gathering myself. Suspecting cold feet at the March shore, the CO suggested I look a little more wholehearted. I did something obscuring with a towel, which the wind assisted from my hands. I stared down the camera's deep eye, his phantom eye behind it, framing me.

When it was developed I autographed the front: *to my dear [character], till death do us part. Your devoted [nom du guerre].* I'll only need the name again when they inform me of his demise. (I mustn't overegg it: bland shock's more credible than desolation, and I've never had a full command of tears.) Someone of the right build accustomed the new uniform to wear. The CO slipped my likeness, pre-distressed, into the coat, to be absolved by the sea. He himself pocketed the personal effects for weeks, taking care to knock off their ingénue sheen before consigning them to their namesake: ticket stubs (Tube and theatre), decoy engagements, the receipt for the ring. My longer letters were drafted in, but I'm entrusted with the incidental notes. To make it more believable, the CO adopts the character and takes me out for cocktails, those red-herring theatre trips.

I avoid the phone, knowing when it rings what to expect.

Melatonin

In the quarry the valley has nibbled the sun
bit by bit until all but the black things are gone.

The cave has extinguished the fidgeting light
and fallen in silence to welcome the night.

The river has swallowed the bulb of the moon
and if you don't watch it'll swallow you soon.

Deep in the forest the day is blown out
so now you can't see what that crying's about.

That dark little spot which appears to be growing –
don't give it a thought. It's probably nothing.

Catherine Crowe's Undoing

She unpacks the trousseau of herself, bonnet first.
The sateen ruffles come apart
at her light touch, spilling her mind.

Next her hair unravels in the sunshine,
spitting pins. Her bone-white collar tumbles
to the mud, the course of hooves.

She looses the microclimates of pagoda sleeves,
disperses confidential heat. The undersleeves,
which together formed a soft embrace,
ease to handshakes, mere acquaintances.

Falling like a curtain at the overture
her overskirt is made immaterial;
the farthingale
stands of its own accord.

Her bloomers wilt. She snaps the corset
open, hook from eye, disclosing
much more than strict baleen should countenance.
She sheds the loosened skin of her chemise.

A neighbour pauses *en route* to buying gloves;
takes pains to notice nothing on this ordinary day.

Miss Crowe stands shivering, invisibility achieved,
but sensible to two remaining needs:
a white lace handkerchief should she sneeze or cry;
her calling cards to tell where she has been.

Oxford, Exterior, Day

In primetime, death is everywhere –
but here location scouts establish
businesses fit for the purpose.

All this materialised in the night.
Streets alter, tricksy as memory.
A taxidermist's has sprung up behind
a frontage – a house with nothing
behind the eyes – and you can't think
what it's replaced.

You breeze through a murder,
eyebrow *can I get through* to
a techie in Converse. He dissolves the puckering crowd
reflected in a pane, unwanted
witnesses to the shot. We mustn't show we're here.
Cobbles, man down: slip a gear.

A likely-looking miscreant slouches
about, lugging a prop
that plays its part: *Stuffed Deer*
as Stuffed Deer among gaffers,
gofers, best boy grips.

Context will be conjured later.
Post-production will force entry
between *here* and TV's *now*.

The detective looks stoic in the gutter
incorrectly, so they shoot
        him again and again.
They've got it all worked out.
        The big reveal's already in the can
and still the muscle in the wraparounds
        stands silent, giving nothing away.

Freaks

The Gray Fossil Museum, Tennessee

Everything that's perished here is notable
either for hugeness
or absurd smallness.

Always some qualifier
denies the creature familiarity
(the 'short-faced' bear, the 'three-
toed' horse, the alarming 'giant' sloth)

as though all the world's anomalies
gathered here before the clock was started
and agreed, to save discomfiture,
to put a stop to themselves.

Now this treacherous Miocene grave,
a sinkhole on the edge of the highway,
gives them away.

Perhaps the governor had the right idea:
bulldoze the lot,
let the freaks disperse anonymous and
uncategorised –

their right-shaped cousins skipping
over the usual soil
with their long faces,
        their five toes, their jeans,
        their hairdos.

Fortune

I

The red sliver of a Christmas fish
bucks and writhes in the heat of a hand.
Curled flanks predict a windfall;
a cocked head warns of jealousy. Flush
to the curve of a cracker, it's easy to miss.

II

My contact lens was misbehaving.
I fished it out and examined it in the cold
of my palm. Inside-out, which explains why
all this time I haven't been able to see
what's staring me in the face.

Moth Season

Brown scraps, they materialise
in edges – curtains, vision, folds
in the bed. I think them into each
cobweb, loose in the peripheries:
killing them is a duty to protect
my woollens, my hand-me-down
silks. There's one like an eyebrow
worrying the wall. I dispense it
with a tissue and an apology, wipe away
the smear of dust. They live in
cracks in the boards, unaccountable,
shrewd witnesses to my life in the
open. I widen a wardrobe gap and
they filter in, plump with eggs and
their own ideas. By night I swear I
hear their working wings, their flitting
between garments. They are always
undecided; they try everything on.

A Shell Family

for Sally, Kate, Sarah and Alex

Mum used to show me how
to stack concentric cockle shells
to make a crinolined lady –
a blank pink cowrie for a face,
her whelk breasts small and armoured,
her parasol a jaunty conch.

Later came the grannyish collection: a running
joke on the mantelpiece. We'd accrue
souvenir trinkets whenever we discovered one:
an owl crusted with ersatz feathers; a fat ship
with sheening mother-of-pearl sails;
the frog family, googly-eyed, conferring in a ring.

They were part of the furniture, outrageous tackiness
turning – eventually – invisible. The glitter-glue
and grubby bowties didn't register until you
really *looked* at them.

And last week I spotted the little crowd
on a glass shelf, priced up for charity,
which makes it even worse.

The Catch

'Candle made from the body of a storm petrel with a wick of tarred string passed through its body. Used by fishermen'
– Pitt Rivers Museum, Oxford

A petrel wobbles
in our wake –
battling its wings'
uselessness.

The lookout hails
into the weather.
We hear no words
but catch his meaning

and lure the sea-ripe bird
with titbits and rope,
full of cunning.
We snap its neck,

feed string
through the open
question of its beak,
push purpose
down its throat;

strike a match and watch the flicker
creep towards the craw, and catch.

We raise the little candle
like St Christopher
against the swelling night.
The mackerel answering light's call
gather at the sea-brink.

We heave the brimming nets,
our silver livelihood –
their eyes all finding out –
and make our way.